PRAYING
IN THE
Safe Room

VICTORIA ROWLAND

Fulton Books, Inc.
Meadville, PA

Published by Fulton Books 2020

ISBN 978-1-64952-097-5 (paperback)
ISBN 978-1-64952-098-2 (digital)

Printed in the United States of America

To my family, I love you beyond words!

Ted, Lance, Leslie and Stetson, Jeff and Meredith, Dan and Lilliona.
Papa Joe and Granny Hattie, Grandma Betty and Sande.
Lilly, Aidan, Landry, Grant, Blakelee, Vivian, and Dovie.
Payton, Kasey, Jimma, Bryson, and Kaeleigh.
Terry, Vanessa, Ben, Abi, and Rebekah.
Wade, Cindy, and Elizabeth.
Zane, Stacie, Judson, Christian, Roman, Charlie, and Allie.
Nick, LeeAnna, Breh and Tresson.

Special thank you to all of my friends and family who
have made my life better by just knowing you.

CHAPTER 1

Tornado Shakes My Faith

When I am afraid, I put my trust in you. (Psalm 56:3)

Praying in a safe room, You were in our presence, shielding us from disaster. I believe Jesus saved my life. May 19, 2015, turned out to be one of the most emotion-filled days of my life. I had traveled to Texas to be present for one the most joyous occasions on earth, the birth of my granddaughter. Watching my baby girl being wheeled back to surgery to have a C-section so that she could deliver her baby girl is beyond emotional. Fear and excitement rolled in one huge ball.

Smooth delivery, as tears of joy stream my face, as I hold God's perfect creation. My daughter and her daughter together as her husband and the rest of the family cherish the incredible moment. I left the hospital elated and did not even really notice the storm clouds on the horizon. Reflexively, I made the forty-five-minute drive to my daughter's home; I know I was not concentrating. My mind was smiling as I was reliving the day. My daughter and her baby were healthy and perfect, just as a birth should be. The doctor part of me thinks of everything that could go wrong, yet I know most of the time complications do not occur. As I pulled up to my daughter's home, the storm clouds were not overly concerning. As I am an Oklahoma girl, tornados and spring storms are very common. I went straight to the nursery, which had been prepared for the baby, a beautifully decorated room. The room had an entire wall that was painted like a Tiffany's package. The ribbon was white, and the accent wall was a perfect Tiffany blue. My daughter had a closet full of clothes and blankets and shoes. She loves shoes. Obviously, the room made me smile, and I could not wait to see the beautiful baby asleep in the crib. My parents (yes, how lucky that a baby is born with not only grandparents but also great-grandparents still alive and fairly healthy) were already in the home along with my daughter/granddaughter, Lilliona. (I will explain that situation later.) The storm continued to rage with rain and hail, and then the sirens. We decided to take cover. The garage had a large walk-in safe, and that is where we went. The sirens' deafening sound warned of the approaching storm.

"Dear Lord Jesus, we ask that you keep us safe. Please, dear Lord, lift the storm over our home and keep us from harm. Please lift it up, Lord, over our roof." We are all holding hands and prayed in unison. As the tornado ravaged through Bridgeport, I sat with my mom, dad, and granddaughter, Lilliona, in a gun safe that we used as a storm shelter. This was the day that my beautiful granddaughter, Blakelee, was born. The storm came as a thief in the night, sucking the oxygen out of the air. The sounds in the house were as if someone was walking and shaking the whole house. In fact, we all kept saying "Is anybody there?" Within a few minutes, all was eerily quiet, but the house was still standing. The tornado came across the yard, lifted above the house, and down on the other side of the yard. When the storm had passed and the house was still standing, my dad said, "We just survived a tornado, and there were five of us in the room instead of four." We all felt God's presence. I am even more sure of the reality of heaven and God's peace when you are battling a storm. Teach your children how to pray. Lilly's sweet six-year-old prayer may be the reason we all survived the tornado. She held on to all of us and said, "We will all be together." When the storm came upon the fishermen, Jesus was there. When death was upon Lazarus, Jesus was there. Jesus will be with you through all trials and storms. Trust in Him.

God's presence is in our lives daily. As He spared our lives, others were not so lucky. A tornado leaves so much destruction, fear, and grief to all those who experience this event.

> Be strong and courageous. Do not be afraid or terrified because of them, for the Lord your God goes with you, He will never leave you or forsake you. (Deuteronomy 31:6)

> I prayed to the Lord and He answered me. He freed me from all my fears. (Psalm 34:4)

> For I am the Lord, your God, who takes hold of your right hand and says to you, "Do Not Fear, I will help you," declares the Lord, your Redeemer, the Holy One of Israel. (Isaiah 41:13–14)

Describing the tornado as a thief in the night brought to my memory the time when my daughter was just a toddler years before when we experienced a real, live thief invasion our home. The experience of the thief in the night will scare a person for a long time. One night, when my children were very small toddlers, I had them tucked in after bedtime stories and hugs and kisses. I decided to go down stairs to do some finishing touches on my kitchen. I did not turn on the lights, just had night-lights glowing. As I opened the laundry room to put a dish towel in the dirty clothes basket, I was pushed and shoved by someone running through my house. I started screaming as he exited another door that lead out to the pool. The children came to the top of the stairs, and I remember yelling to them to go back upstairs as I called the police. The boy lost his hat in the kitchen when he gave me a little push. The police came and searched the neighborhood. They found no trace of the boy but found my purse thrown on the street the next block over. My wallet was found, missing only my money. The terror felt for months of knowing someone had invaded our home is difficult to describe. Prior to that night, we all felt so secure, and after that night, every sound evoked a very eerie, scary feeling. I often think of this young boy and pray that he has found God's light. Walking in God's lighted path is more rewarding than sneaking around in total darkness. This book is about a few events that God showed up and held my hand. Every second of every day, God is present. I am an imperfect child of God, hoping with certainty that God can use my life and the knowledge He has given me to help someone in need.

CHAPTER 2

My Christian Walk Begins

He is the one you praise; he is your god, who performed
for you those great and awesome wonders you saw
with your own eye. (Deuteronomy 10:21)

L ife is full of frightful events. I have weathered not only the tornado but many other events where God was present, holding my hand to help me through. I was born in 1962 in a small Oklahoma town. My parents had to kneel in prayer early in my life because I developed pyloric stenosis within a few days of being born. This condition, normally found in boys, causes projectile vomiting and dehydration, and starvation quickly ensues if not treated. Pyloric stenosis is now easily recognized with all the testing capabilities, but back then it was quite a bit more challenging. After several different doctor visits, finally a surgeon said it was too late and I might not survive the corrective surgery, but my mom went to her knees in prayer, and my dad brought the priest. Both of my parents said, "Perform the surgery." Prayer brought the right surgeon, and I know God was holding his hands through the procedure. As He spared my life as an infant, I remember my mom saying many times that I was God's child. Sometime in elementary school, I attended a children's crusade in my hometown with some of my classmates. I remember my classmate Becky stepped out boldly when a call for salvation was pronounced by the preacher. I, on the other hand, was scared to go forward but followed her lead. Kneeling in prayer that day, I received forgiveness from God and started my journey with God. Forty years later, I saw a Facebook post by that same Becky that said a person becomes ten times more attractive not by looks but by the acts of kindness, respect, honor, loyalty, and love they show. Obviously, God's grace and love is still working miracles in her heart as she still reaches humbly to follow God's plan. We may never even know someone is watching, listening, or following our path.

For all who want God's gift of salvation and to receive God's grace, love, and peace, the prayer is very simple.

> Who can be saved? Jesus looked at the disciples and said, "With man this is impossible, but with God all things are possible." (Matthew 19:25–26)

That you confess with your mouth, "Jesus is Lord," and believe with your heart that God raised Him from the dead, you will be saved. For it is with your heart that you believe and are justified, and it is with your mouth that you confess and are saved. (Romans 10:9–10)

The spirit and the bride say. "Come!" Let the one who is thirsty come and let the one who wishes to take the gift of the water of life. (Revelation 22:17)

You cannot enter heaven with good works. It is a gift! When all you know is a life of sin, it is hard to believe that following God will make you happier than any high you receive from Satan's destructive forces, such as drugs or alcohol.

My childhood existed in rural Oklahoma, where life had a much slower pace than it does today. My grandparents owned a chicken farm and raised cattle. They also planted a very large garden every summer and spent countless hours planting, harvesting, and canning the produce. Some of my favorite memories as a child include the times of being in to the watermelon patch with my Daddy Ted (grandfather) as he would teach us how tell if the watermelon was ripe. He would thump them and take out his pocketknife and cut them open, and we would taste them. He cut open many watermelons and let us eat all we wanted. Most of the time, we just ate the heart of the melon, and he would then get another one and see if it was ripe. My Moma Katherine (grandmother) was known as the biscuit maker. Her recipe was two cups of self-rising flour, two tablespoons of shortening, and one and one-fourth cup of buttermilk. Mix and cut into one-inch biscuits. Put bacon grease in pan and dip to top the biscuits in grease and place in pan. Bake at four hundred twenty-five degrees until lightly brown. She made corn bread or biscuits for almost every meal. Sorghum syrup sat on the table to be available whenever a sweet tooth struck. Our family gatherings were almost always centered around a big meal. My mom and all her sisters could cook and would bring the best desserts and snacks to our events. Cousin time was so special. Because of these special times, we can spend years apart and can immediately hold a conversation when we are reunited.

When we would go to town to deliver all the eggs that we had gathered, Moma Katherine and Daddy Ted would let me get candy for all the cousins. I would pick giant pixie sticks, and she always made sure I got one for all her grandchildren. On the way back from our trip from town, Daddy Ted would stop by almost every house that lived on our Union Grove road and visit. Many times our neighbors and all our relatives would be sitting on their front porches. Most people waved at each other, but not my grandfather. He would pull in and talk for a while. We might not even get out of the truck, but he took the time to say a proper hello. Great memories as a child playing games, playing in the mud, riding horses, riding bicycles, running outside, and having special bonds are still present today because of these family gatherings.

My dad grew up in Iowa, and over the last few years, his childhood cousins have been re-acquainted through family reunions. It is such a joy to see them all laugh and listen to their childhood stories. They describe playing in the snow and having great food provided by Grandma Victoria. My grandmother, of whom I was named after, never forgot a birthday or Christmas. She, like my Aunt Sister Immacula, made every holiday special because it was so exciting to receive a card in the mail. She made homemade bread with raisins. The smell of fresh yeast bread baking in the oven was a memory they all shared. My dad delivered newspapers and remembers a doughnut store giving him doughnuts while he was on his route. And as a young boy he thought those doughnuts were the best. Iowa mornings could be cold and dark while riding a bicycle at 5:00 a.m., but the doughnuts seemed to make the job less frightful. My dad was raised in a very religious Catholic home. My grandmother prayed for all her ten children and all the extended family. We continue her faithful prayers. When anything strikes our family, we get on the hotline of social media, and the whole family sends prayers. The clan is huge! When God is bombarded with this whole family's unified prayer, I often wonder what He thinks. Does He smile? Does He say "Oh no, not them again"? LOL. My dad joined the Air Force, and his other three brothers served in the Marine and the Army. This noble, kind family is blessed. God is continually pouring his favor on this praying, united family. The whole family has experienced trials, but the knees bow down together as we pray for each other in unison. My extended family includes many aunts, uncles, and cousins. All hold a special place in my heart, and each have their own set of memories. It is very fortunate to live with praying grandparents, parents, and family. Family should be an important aspect of life. Try to bridge disagreements, keep close to your relatives, and call each other.

In the Old Testament, there are many words describing family lineages. Ever wonder why so many chapters in the Bible were dedicated to the lineage? These strange verses are so hard to read, and keeping it straight is almost impossible. I even drew a family tree of the Bible names starting with the book of Genesis and wanted to study it, but so many facts and difficult names makes it hard to grasp. As I reflect on my family and the importance of all of them, the remnant of Jesus Christ's lineage described in the Bible has a new meaning as well. It is so important to protect your family name with honesty and get back to a time when your word meant something. My Aunt Nell used to make my favorite peanut butter fudge often, and when she died, my Aunt Claudean started delivering this wonderful treat to me every Christmas. This fudge is the best ever, but more importantly, it reminds me of how special our memories and family traditions continue to be. Another of my special treats is given to me by my Aunt Lu: homemade pickles. They are some of the best pickles and remind me of Marie (Nana) Pardue's hot mustard pickles. Aunt Lu brings the pickles to my workplace, and many of the employees, including my daughter, seem to need a pickle a day. Recently, my cousin Yoli started making caramel apples that turned out to be our favorite dessert at Thanksgiving. My mom's caramel pie is incredible and she continues the the tradition of both of my grandmothers biscuits and homemade yeast rolls, Grandma Betty's chicken and dressing and banana pudding, Papa's macaroni and cheese, Mama Katherine's tea cookies, my husband's ribs, my brothers salsa, my son-in-law's barbecue anything, my brother-in-law's jambalaya, my friend Tammie's snacks of all kinds but especially anything spicy, my gooey popcorn, my daughter's buffalo cheese dip, Cindy's broccoli and cheese casserole, Vanessa's taco soup, LeeAnna's corn casserole, Stacie's puppy chow, Granny Sue's pumpkin pie, Sandy and Althea's banana pudding, and my friend's baked macaroni and cheese top of some of our Southern comfort family traditions. With all these great foods, I wonder why I have such a hard time controlling my weight. Just having all these wonderful foods in our life brings special bonds for our whole family. Every holiday, as we get together as a family, prior to consuming all these mouthwatering foods, we stand together, holding hands in a very large circle, and ask God's blessing on our meal and give thanks for His many blessings. Our cabin traditions are riding four wheelers, taking pictures on the cliff, fishing, and playing many games. We especially love playing spades. The family that I cherish is truly a blessing that God has bestowed upon my life in such a way that I hope I never take for granted.

To go through life without God's presence and Him to lean on in troubling times seems almost impossible to me. As I walk through life, I have watched one dream after another come into my life. I always wanted to be a doctor and worked hard to achieve this dream. Brother Brett Miller preached a sermon about dreaming big one Sunday morning when he talked about Genesis 37:6, which said, "Listen to this dream I had. We were binding sheaves of grain out in the field when my sheaf rose and stood upright, while your sheaves gathered around mine and bowed down to it." This is Joseph talking to his older brothers who hated him and even more so after that dream. They never would bow to their younger brother, but they did, and God allowed Joseph to be sold into slavery to save the remnant of the Jews, which was the lineage of Jesus.

The Bible teaches of the importance of brotherly love and forgiveness. Obviously, sometimes our brothers mistreat us, as did Joseph's, but when he had the chance, he forgave them and protected them. Not everyone or everything will be exactly fair, but God has a plan and will put you exactly where you need to be if you will just follow His lead.

The world can be hard to maneuver by yourself. Back when I played basketball, with six girls on a team and played half-court, the coach used the adage "No pain, no gain." Now, few use this saying, but something that is still taught today by many coaches and leaders is the importance of teamwork. Many of my basketball teammates are still my best friends to this day. Team sports may often have a superstar, but that superstar needs a whole team if they ever want to be a winner. I was never a superstar when it came to sports, but I worked hard to do my best for our team. God does not pick everyone to kill Goliath or to become king, but every person is important. Even the woman at the well, who was so ashamed to be seen, was used by God to deliver a very important message. A true star is someone who humbly follows God's lead and maybe never even receives any praise on earth, but God is watching your sweet moves. My son played basketball for a small school, and he was not the best player on the team. The best player on the team, who was incredible, decided he was going to make sure every player made some points. I watched in amazement as this young boy, who could score almost every time the ball was in his hands, pass the ball off to his teammates, my son included, until they had all scored. While he was a hero to the school for his great athletic talents, he was more of a hero as he helped the teammates feel important and appreciated. I have no memory of how many points he scored per game other than it was a lot, but I remember this one special game forever as he bestowed true friendship on my son. Funny thing about small gestures that you do not give a second thought about is that it can be a turning point in someone's life. Kindness is described as one of the fruits of the spirit.

> But the fruit of the Spirit is love, joy, peace, patience, kindness, goodness, faithfulness, gentleness, self-control, against such things there is no law. (Galatians 5:22–23)

> Remember the words of the Lord Jesus how he himself said, "It is more blessed to give than to receive." (Acts 20:35)

> Put on them, as God's chosen ones, holy,
> beloved, compassionate hearts, kindness, humil-
> ity, meekness, and patience. (Colossians 3:12)

Sometimes it is hard to know if you are following God's will in your life's journey or if you are just doing what you want. I had one of those feelings as I went off to college. While I had been a Christian for several years and worked hard at remembering every bone in the body and learning chemical properties for my next chemistry test for one of the most awesome teachers in the world, I spent very little time memorizing Bible verses. I, in fact, only knew one Bible verse outside the shortest verse, "Jesus wept" (John 11:35). The verse I knew was Galatians 2:20, which says "I am crucified with Christ, nevertheless I live, yet not I, but Christ lives in me and the life which I now live in the flesh, I live by the faith of the Son of God who loved me and gave himself for me." Why I learned this verse, I had no idea, but it was placed in my heart to memorize. Therefore, I did. Not the easiest verse, but after several days, it was etched in my heart forever. I had butterflies in the pit of my stomach as I arrived to my college dorm room to meet my roommates. They all seemed super nice. One was a chemistry major just like myself, one was just plain nice to the bone, and one was a preacher's daughter whose favorite Bible verse hung in her room. What was it? You guessed it. Galatians 2:20. God was preparing me for this very moment months before it happened, and I believe He was also helping his precious Carla as well. I relaxed after our first day together and my time in college including dorm life was great. While working on a research project in college, our group got accepted to go to Washington, DC, to do a science presentation. The weekend of the presentation was the weekend that the MCAT was given, which is the entrance exam that must be taken before you can apply to medical school. Since my dad was from Iowa, I had traveled out of Oklahoma, but never by myself. However, everything worked out perfectly. I gave my presentation, and then one of dad's cousins who lived in the DC area came to our hotel in Washington, DC, and took me to the school where I tested all day, and then he returned me to the hotel. Today, the college kids are more travel-savvy than

I was then. As I reflect back on that time, I know God's hand was there helping me through that weekend. Think about taking one of the hardest tests of your life in a strange place while preparing for a huge science presentation on copper chelation, which is used to help find a cure/treatment for Wilson's disease. What are the odds that it all came off perfectly? The day of the MCAT was the day the rest of the scientist did the Washington, DC, tour. After that, we traveled back to our Oklahoma campus, and one of the scientists attending the presentation contacted the school and offered a classmate and myself a summer job in Lawrence Livermore National Laboratory near San Francisco, California. We both went. He ended up staying there after college, and I returned to graduate. I graduated in three years and was accepted into medical school.

I will never forget my first day of medical school when one of the instructors asked for a show of hands as to who attended church regularly. I, of course, raised my hand boldly, and then he said before this semester is over, you will not be in church. You will not go out with friends, you will not go to the movies, and you will not do anything fun. My thought at that very moment was *You are so wrong. I will be in church!* However, he was right. Within the first few weeks, the courses totally consumed every waking hour. I routinely went to bed at 10:00 p.m. to wake up at 2:00 a.m. every morning to study. I have since had this conversation with a physician who attended medical school in India, and he laughed as he said that was his exact hours as well. We are business partners for the last twenty years and again believe that God was preparing my life's journey and placing the right people in my path.

Just as I was entering my fourth year of medical school, I received some unwelcome news. I found out that I was pregnant. My first thought was of how I could complete school with a baby. As the shock started to wear off and I started to get excited about the new life growing inside me, the unthinkable happened. I started bleeding. Everyone told me that I was miscarrying and that I should have a D and C. I could not believe it. My guilt was consuming my every thought. It was obviously my fault because I was not excited about the baby. The doctor strongly urged me to terminate the pregnancy. I was determined to keep this baby. He warned me that bleeding could get very heavy. In the middle of the night, the floodgates opened up, and my hemorrhaging was unstoppable. I had lost the baby.

Medical school consumed every waking hour, and it was my life's dream. The demanding career took my focus away from God, and I ended up divorced with two small children. My career path was exactly where I wanted to be, but I felt like a complete failure in my personal life. With this failure, I was embarrassed and again pulled away from God when I should have been the closest to Him.

CHAPTER 3

God's Signs and Healing Power

God also testified to it by signs, wonders and various miracles, and by gifts of the Holy Spirit distributed according to his will. (Hebrews 2:4)

My journey with God by my side has proven to be so incredible. Once I was walking in the beautiful mountains along Buck Creek in a small Oklahoma town, just praying with tears streaming down my face and asking God, "Please show me a sign that You are there!" One of my dear patients once said that God knows the desires of our heart, and He knows what is important to you and will answer your prayers no matter how unimportant they may seem to someone else. If it is important to us, it is important to God. That being said, anyone familiar with this very rural country knows that deer sheds are found often, but I personally had never found one and had often went looking. As I was hiking through the woods, praying for a sign from God, I remember thinking to myself, *God, let me find a deer shed today, please, so that I know that You are with me.* At my very next step, I looked down, and I was standing on a single point deer horn. The biggest smile came to my face as I realized that God had a baby buck walk in that exact spot and lose its single pointed horn just for me to find at the exact time that I needed God's touch. When I thanked God for this miracle, I realized that if I were in charge of the deer, I would have probably had the biggest buck in the forest drop a full twenty-point rack, not the smallest horn in the woods. As I think back on this moment, I know that if the biggest horn were present, I would not have been completely convinced that it was a sign from God. Many people can find big horns, but it was the small horn that was exactly what I needed in order to remember that day, and my smile reflected on just how much God loved me and how important my dreams are to Him.

Around this time, I herniated a disk in my C-spine (aka neck). My MRI revealed the disc abnormality, and my pain was ten out of ten. I literally had to have help to get dressed, and my left hand was going numb and tingling. I was scheduled for surgery, and on the morning of the surgery, I felt like my body would break when I tried to move. We live three hours away from the hospital that was to perform my surgery, and I remember the drive up as almost unbearable. I was on the hospital bed being wheeled back to surgery when I asked my husband, daughter, mom, and dad if the nurse had given me anything in my IV because the pain was gone. They all said they did not think that I had received anything. When the neurosurgeon approached, I asked him if I had received anything for and pain, and he said no. I sat up and announced that my pain was gone. I decided to not have the surgery and went home. Even though I was not scheduled to work the following day because I was supposed to be recovering from surgery, I felt perfect and decided to go and see any walk-ins that might need to be seen that day. My first patient was a beautiful, gentle Christian lady whom I attended church with several years earlier, and she said, "I have been praying for you. God just laid you on my mind." I thanked her for her prayers and said nothing else. The next patient was another lady who said, "I prayed for you the last few days." Again, I said thank you, told her that my neck had been hurting, and assured her that I appreciated her prayers. I was starting to realize that God had healed me, and He had random Christians praying for me. The third patient was the town drunk. I smiled as I entered the room as I was sure that God had sent him for me to comfort in some way or another, but I was wrong. The man said, "I prayed for you two nights ago. I bet you think since I am a drunk that God does not hear my prayers, but He does. I don't know what is wrong with you, but God has it under control." I no longer think that my neck just got better. God healed me, and to this day almost twenty years later, I have no pain in my neck. My hand strength is perfect, and no numbness or tingling exists. In addition, I use no medication. God also showed me that each and every one of God's creations has a purpose, and I am reminded of how we are not perfect, but God can use all of us, great or not so great, in His perfect plan.

God loves us and looks out for us. This became very apparent to me when our small hospital had an auditor come down from Oklahoma City to watch six mammograms to be performed. The administrator from the hospital called over to our clinic around noon and said they needed six volunteers to come to the hospital right then to get a free mammogram with the auditor present. Therefore, of course, I told the hospital administrator I would send six females over. Turning to my nurse's station, I pointed to three of my nurses and said that the hospital needed them over in X-ray department to get a free mammogram. My office manager and assistant manager was in the hall talking to me about some clinic business when the hospital called back and said they still needed three more volunteers. My manager said that our lab technician had not gone to lunch, and she said she could go. I then turned to the assistant manager and said for her to go get her mammogram. She looked me squarely in the eye to inform me that she was not old enough to get the screening mammogram. We had five sent over, it was now lunchtime, and the clinic was empty. The hospital still needed one more. That left one person—me. I agreed to go as they proceeded to tell me to go to registration and then go to X-ray department, and that is when I said that I was too busy. I was still seeing morning patients and just could not spare the time. A few minutes later, the hospital called back to tell me that all the paperwork at registration had been completed for me and that all I had to do was go straight to mammogram and that I was going in front of everyone else so I could get back to the clinic. Therefore, I went. Doctors make the worst patients because I was only sixteen years overdue for a mammogram. I went back to work and did not give the exam a second thought. The next morning, I get a phone call telling me that my mammogram had some calcifications that looked suspicious and that I needed a spot compression. I realized that I had walked out of the X-ray department without even looking at my films. My first reaction was that I am going to look at my films and decide if I was going to have any more tests. The next morning, after completing rounds at the hospital, I looked at the film and thought it was nothing, but I will do the spot. This time, when the test was completed, I wanted to see my x ray. The technician turned the blown up screen so I could see my film, and pure panic mode developed. As I left the hospital, tears started streaming, I just wanted to be alone and have the world stop for a few minutes so I could catch my breath. Later that day, the final report was called to me, and it came back BI-RADS 4B with a seventy to eighty percent chance of malignancy. Being in practice for thirty years has its disadvantages when you are getting reports on yourself. Knowing that this particular strand of calcified clusters is usually associated with cancer made for a frightful day. Unlike when my neck was hurt and God sent people to pray for me without even asking, I immediately turned to God for comfort. The ride from being the doctor to becoming the patient had begun. Obviously up to this point, I had received VIP treatment. The next step was getting a biopsy scheduled. One doctor was on vacation and finally called on a dear cardiologist who got a biopsy scheduled right away in his town. Through the years, this doctor has been so responsive to all my patients' needs, and he did not disappoint when I was the one in need of fast professional care. With the biopsy completed and repeat mammogram done, I went home to wait on the results. The doctor called as soon as the biopsy was back, and she informed me that she had taken fourteen separate biopsies, and all were negative for cancer. As I was sighing a sigh of relief, she said but. She then said that she was sure she missed the cancer because she really felt like it was cancer, and the new radiologist had upgraded my repeat mammogram from a 4B to a 4C, which holds a 90 percent chance of malignancy.

As I discussed my case with the surgeon, we decided that the next best course of action was to undergo a lumpectomy. This procedure was scheduled for the following week. A few weeks earlier in our small town, we had a deer festival. It is like a typical small town carnival. Kids love riding the miniature ponies, and the tree carving is always fun to watch. How they take a piece of wood and turn it into a piece of art is unbelievable. As we visited all the booths, I had donated to one of the veterans' booths. The lady at the booth knew me and filled out my chances with the money I had donated. During this rocky time in my life, facing the fight of a lifetime, I received a call from the veteran's organization stating that they had drawn my name weeks ago but had not been able to get in touch with me. I had won a gun, a case, and a scope. The lady asked if she could deliver it to me that day, and of course, she wanted to take my picture with the prize. I have shot a handgun once or twice in my life and know absolutely nothing about guns, but it is always exciting to win. The lady who delivered the gun just happened to be the wife of my past pastor. As soon as I saw this retired preacher's wife, I jumped at the opportunity to ask for prayer for my abnormal mammogram. She, of course, said she would and assured me that she and her husband would keep me in prayer. I know many people off the cuff say things like "I will pray for you" and never give it a second thought. I can say I am even guilty of this, and so now whenever I tell someone that I will pray for them, I try to do it immediately so I won't forget. However, this precious couple who walked through life teaching God's Word did not forget. A few days later, as luck would have it (or as I like to think), God arranged for me to run into this pastor. It was like the two of us in this big parking lot, and he said he was hoping that he would see me and prayed with me right on the spot. He looked at me and said "You are going to be all right" after he finished praying. On the day of the surgery, a visit from a doctor friend surprised me, with several praying warriors from his church who prayed feverishly over me before I was taken back to surgery. The surgery went great, and no cancer was found. For all of you fighting cancer or back pain or whatever it is that you are facing, wondering why God does not heal you, I do not have the answers. I do know that God is walking with you during this trial in your life

Recently on a ski trip to Breckenridge, Colorado, with all my children and grandchildren, I was enjoying one of the most peaceful mornings on the ski slope I had ever witnessed. As I rode the lift up for the third time that morning, I sat in prayer, praising God for my family and the beautiful scenery. The view of the snow-topped mountains with the sun shining and reflecting the most incredible glistening vision put a broad smile across my face. At that moment, I could not have been closer to God. God has made some amazing, awesome scenery, and the snow-topped mountains in Breckenridge are among some of His greatest masterpieces. For all non-skiers, the ride up the lift can be long and cold, but this morning, it was not. There was no wind, and the sun was shining brightly, warming the ride up to make it a perfect temperature. As I prepared to unload from the lift, everything seemed perfect and peaceful. Riding on a six-person lift, I was positioned on the right outside seat. As my husband and I stood to get off the lift, he hit ice and skied right in front of me, and I fell down. The pop in my knee and the pain that ensued was excruciating. I realized fairly quickly after attempting to stand that my knee was injured. While lying in the snow and waiting for paramedics to arrive so I could take the embarrassing ride down the mountain on a stretcher, I remember thinking why was this allowed by God? Why did this happen? I had just been enjoying such a peaceful perfect moment in His presence, and then I realized He showed up to be there for me when I fell. I tore my ACL, MCL, and patella femoral ligaments and had surgery to repair the knee. After a great orthopedic surgeon in Tulsa performed my surgery perfectly, I had the opportunity to visit my sister-in-law and her wonderful staff for a bout of physical therapy. After grueling therapy sessions, and even though I have been a doctor for thirty years, I realize I do not have enough sympathy for my patients with knee injuries requiring knee surgery. This was and continues to be most challenging. The loss of independence as I required help to get dressed, take a shower, and prepare meals was quite upsetting. I had fourteen steps to go in my front door and had to be wheeled up a very steep ramp to get in my home and required the same assistance to leave the house, which my husband and daughter and many others did without complaints. I hated to ask anyone for help, and hopefully this experience will help me help someone else.

The trial that confronts a person and his or her family while battling an illness may be the hardest time in anyone's life. Illness brings us all to our knees. Facing the unknown outcome of an illness or enduring any medical hardships brings the total realization that we have to have God at that moment. The comfort of God's presence is the only way that medical situations can be faced. This became very apparent when my eighty-one-year-old dad calls one evening stating that he was having a chest pain that would not go away. My daughter and her husband lives closest to my parents, so they went and got Dad, and we met in the ER. His cardiac enzymes elevated a little, so I called on the greatest cardiovascular surgeon I know, who arranged to get my dad to the city. Dad underwent a heart catheterization, which revealed significant blockage, and he was scheduled for an open-heart surgery the following morning. Again, doctor knowledge gets in the way when you start thinking of all possibilities. As my dad was wheeled back, emotions started to flood my soul. Our entire family called every prayer warrior that we knew, and the beautiful little nurse who had helped with dad's heart catheterization showed up with doughnuts. How sweet she was to us all. Then that same praying doctor that showed up for my biopsy a few years earlier also showed up for support through this six-hour surgery on my dad. Everything went smoothly, and just as he was going to be released from the ICU, COVID-19 scare hits. This was on a Friday, and on Monday, the hospital was stopping all visitors, except at certain times. How hard it was to think about leaving him alone the first night we had to leave the hospital. I was so thankful that he was recovering instead of just having surgery without all of us present. Dad was released from the hospital, and about one week later, his brother was diagnosed with COVID-19 in New Jersey. Therefore, here we go again, praying fervently for our family. The Bible mentions so many miracles performed by Jesus: fed thousands with manna, drew water out of a rock, parted the Red Sea, restored the blind's vision, caused the deaf to hear and the lame to walk, cured leprosy, and most importantly, raised the dead back to life. The most important message is that Jesus today still performs miracles every day and is listening to our prayers. The prayers of everyone are sent and received by God, and He pours out His grace and love to us in all situations.

The "Footprints in the Sand" passage is always so inspiring and helps so many overcome horrific situations. Jesus is carrying you through.

> Come to me, all you who are weary and burdened and I will give you rest. Take my yoke upon you and learn from me, for I am gentle and humble in heart, and you will find rest for your souls. (Matthew 11:28)

Life flies by so quickly. The middle part of our life is so full of labor; it is sometimes difficult to find time for the joys of life. Children have few worries, but as life gets more complicated, the burden gets heavy. The answer is so simply outlined in the first book of the New Testament. Jesus will give you rest. Ask and seek Him continually for guidance. If you take your eyes off Him and things go wrong, do not be ashamed. Go back immediately so that you do not miss years of wandering in life with no purpose. If you are a parent, you know the depths of your love for your child, and that being said, there is no limit on how much you love them and what you would do for them. God is so much better than you are, and His depth of love for you and your children are truly endless.

CHAPTER 4

The Flood

The rains fell, and the floods came, and the winds blew
and beat on that house, but it did not fall, because it
had been founded on the rock. (Matthew 7:25)

As I said earlier, I have fourteen steps leading up to my front door, and the reason that I do is because a flood came while we were sleeping with absolutely no warning. Well, that is not exactly true! Our family cabin was built on a beautiful babbling creek, where on a good portion of the year, you can drive a four-wheeler across and barely get the tires wet. Before we owned the land, we used to ride ATVs along the creek, and I would always stop at the bend in the creek and stare. It was one the most beautiful places on earth. The creek had a large mountain cliff view in the background. When the land became for sale, we bought it, and our cabin came to life. The cabin was built on piers, and through the years, the water had gotten close, high and raging but never came in our home. After living here for several years, we could gauge when the river would flood the banks. It usually took a five-inch rain over a very quick time. The night of the flood was not typical. Our family was getting ready to go on a family trip to Disney World. We are campers. My husband is all about camping and traveling to RV parks. Therefore, for us to go to Disney, we all had reservations at the RV Park in Disney World. We were all packed and ready to leave, food in fridge, generators full of gas, and campers hooked up and ready to pull out the next morning. We were taking several RVs, and my husband, our do-everything helpers, Stoney and Maria, and myself worked tirelessly to make the trip perfect for all the children and grandchildren. We were ready to leave early the following morning as we were awakened by my husband's alarm on his phone giving a flash flood warning. My husband grabbed his phone to read the message from the emergency sound. He looked, and not one drop of rain had fallen outside. This was around midnight. Even though we were leaving very early the next day, we were not ready to leave at midnight, so we both went back to sleep, only to have the alarm buzz again a few minutes later. This time, when my husband got up to check, he gently said, "Get up. Water is in the house." When I stood up from my bed, water was already a couple of feet deep. I got Lilly and took her upstairs. Oddly, we still had electricity. It was very scary walking through the rising floodwater that covered the electric sockets as we were trying to get to safety. I grabbed my phone as I made it to the stairs and sat at the top of the stairs with Lilliona, watching the water rise and pour in our home, thinking and wondering when it will stop. I took a picture of the water coming up the stairs and called my son and his wife, who were staying in our guest cabin for the night. I told them to go upstairs, and they wanted to know why. I remember telling them to look outside, and as they looked out the window, they watched their car float away. I then called my daughter to tell her that I loved her just in case anything happened to me and asked her to start a prayer chain. She did all right. I believe she called everyone she knew. Realize this is about two in the morning. The water rose for a while, and by sunrise, there was no water, just the destruction. I remember walking in what was my front driveway now laced with dead fish. As friends and family arrived to help, I sat staring in disbelief. Some dear friends who volunteer with the Baptist Church looked at my face and said that I looked the same as others they had witnessed when natural disaster had struck, a complete look of loss. So many came to help that day. I cannot even imagine having to bear this event alone. Everyone would come up to me with different objects destroyed in my mind. I would look at it and tell them to throw it away. If you have ever encountered a flood, you understand the filth that comes with the raging waters. The tears rolled as each personal belonging was held before me, and I repeatedly told them to throw it away. The mud, trash, and stench that came through the house were horrible. Somehow, we all kept working. I was the least effective of everyone. Everywhere I turned, looking one place to another, everything was ruined. My clothes, shoes, rugs, pictures, furniture, and vehicles were destroyed. I distinctly remember telling one person after another to just throw the item away. It was so dirty that it could never be useful again, but the next morning, my clothes appeared all clean and laundered. They were folded perfectly. These women had taken the time to come help all day and do my laundry all evening. They saw value with these filthy objects and washed them spotless. The returned clothes were perfect without a stain. They had been made complete again. Jesus did the same for us. We are full of sin—too filthy to be used, worthless, and filled with stains—but Jesus sees our value and can wash our sins away. And with complete forgiveness, we are washed white as snow, flawless and purpose-filled. God smiles when we turn to Him and ask for forgiveness. Those clothes were special to me and allowed me to appreciate my family and friends who were there helping me. Would God not want us to do the same for His people? No one is too bad. God sees the good and can cover the sins with the blood of Jesus. As Christians, it is important to not judge the sinner but to show love whenever we can. All our campers were destroyed, but somehow, we were able to go on our vacation a couple of days later. One after another volunteered the use of their camper. Therefore, with borrowed campers, we went on our trip. We were banned from entering our home while the fans and some chemicals were placed to prevent molding. My husband carried a big burden on our vacation, but we were so thankful that no life was lost and things can be replaced. Even our family dog returned, wet and exhausted from his ride down the river.

As we reflect on this flood, we realize that this was at a water level of a fifty-year flood. In fact, I'm not sure if the water has ever been that high before. Therefore, we raised our house almost five feet in hopes to avoid this situation again, and that is how I get to walk up fourteen steps to go in my front door. God told Noah to build an ark, and God flooded the whole earth. Noah and his family along with animals of all walks of life were saved in this devastation.

> I establish my covenant with you. Never again will all life be destroyed by the waters of a flood; never again, will there be a flood to destroy the earth. (Genesis 9:11)

As the water was rising, the people on earth must have felt the fear. The cries that must have come from their mouths. I often wonder if their cries and suffering was the reason God said never again. Even if we are walking totally away from God, when we cry, He hears and cries as well.

As a survivor of a flood, knowledge of God's presence firsthand during this event brings tears of joy with the realization of just how powerful God's outreach in our life encompasses. While the house has been raised and made stronger, a flood brings terror with crushing speed. God can change the course of the river, like the parting of the Red Sea. God can change the course of your life to put you in the exact place for your existence. My dream career was to be a doctor, and God allowed that to happen.

CHAPTER 5

My Walk as a Doctor

Jesus answered them, "It is not the healthy who
need a doctor, but the sick." (Luke 5:31)

I practice medicine in a small rural Oklahoma town and have been blessed to deliver health care to some amazing people. My son Lance was used in God's plan when he was only four years old. As I loaded my two children in the car to go to our regular church, my son started throwing a fit to go to a small church that was right by our house. I, of course, said, "No, we are going to our church." The next Sunday morning, same fit but even stronger. This week I stopped and took both children out of the car seats (anyone with children knows the trouble involved with this feat). As I was walking in this country Baptist church, I thought to myself that it was crazy to let a four-year-old dictate where we went to church. Therefore, I loaded them back in the car, car seats buckled, and went to my church. The next Sunday, same thing happened. The fit started the second he saw the church. He begged and pleaded for me to go to this church. Therefore, I went. I sat on the back row with my two babies. As soon as the preacher started preaching, he said, "I have had this same sermon ready for three weeks now and almost gave it last Sunday, but at the last minute, God had me deliver a different sermon, and finally today, He wants me to deliver the sermon He gave me three weeks ago." Tears rolled down from my eyes since I knew that message was for me. I never attended that church again, my son never asked to go back, and we resumed back to our regular church.

Many years later, I had the opportunity to be this preacher's doctor. He became very sick and was depressed as he looked back on his life. He wondered if he had ever really pleased God. He said that he wanted to believe that he had listened and preformed God's work. Then he looked me squarely in the eyes and said, "But I am not sure." A smile came across my face as I relived the story of the day that I attended his church. I assured him that he had helped me and how he had obeyed God's commands even when he was not sure. He received such peace from this story. I am sure he helped so many more people than just me, but God chose the preacher to deliver a message to me so that on his deathbed I could reassure him of how much God loved him. Ironically, if it was not for a small obedient child being disobedient, I would not have received my personal message from God, and this preacher might have gone to his grave not sure of his life's purpose.

So many patients have been instrumental in my walk with God, like the three praying patients with my herniated disc healing or the patients who send flowers just because. Almost every time, the flowers reflect perfect timing, giving me the bright spot I need for that day. As a rural doctor, I have received gifts as extravagant as a Louis Vuitton wallet to as simple as a homemade card colored by a most special child with everything in between, such as cards, cookies, pies, fudge, jelly, snacks, deer jerky, peppermint candy, chocolate, lotion, hand sanitizers of all flavors, jewelry, cross stitch pictures, complete meals, candy, eggs, home grown tomatoes, plums, blackberries, squash, quilts, homemade table runners, crocheted pot holder, pickles, mango water from Sonic, and the list goes on and on. In addition, I do not want to forget the precious child who said "Can I have a hug?" Caring for the sick is rewarding beyond measure, but also exhausting. Medical care is twenty-four seven, and sometimes health care providers walk in the room at the risk of their own lives. I am married to a physician as well, and so medicine almost never shuts off at our house. Rural America requires endless energy and sacrifice to feel like you are doing a marginal job at best. I often describe our office as McDonald's with a school bus at all times. Sometimes you feel like walking out the back door never to return. The patients complain of long waits, and some are so ungrateful and sometimes just downright rude. Mixed in with the complainers though are the incredible, kind, sympathetic, praying patients that make your day all worthwhile. How many days have my staff and myself gone without breakfast, lunch, or even a bathroom break? How many nights have we been awakened to discuss a case or give orders for these very same patients to hear only complaints that you have not done enough or that their time is more valuable than waiting on the doctor to arrive? Almost never do these patients ask if the hospital let you sleep any last night or the nursing home or if, heaven forbid, your own family needs something, like your father is having an open-heart surgery or your grandchild is sick all night. However, there are those patients who do ask "How are you?" One patient would say, "Sit down and rest while you are in here with me." Others almost always lead to a conversation about God and what miracles have been placed in their life lately. It was truly an honor and privilege to hear the treasured moments in each of their lives. Then just when you have had enough, you have a patient on his deathbed, and you have the opportunity to ask him if he is ready for God. In particular, one patient was in end-stage heart failure and without any insurance and no money. As I sat with him, letting him know there was nothing else that I could do, I asked if he knew God as his Lord and Savior. He looked me square in the eyes and said he was not ready to die. We discussed options, and the only thing left to consider was a heart transplant. This was almost twenty years ago in the early 2000s. Heart transplants were rare and reserved for patients with good insurance because of the cost, and even the cost of the anti-rejection medication was several thousand dollars a month. He asked me to try. Therefore, I started the referral process, and as always God's perfect timing occurred. He was completely bedridden and days from death when the call came and he received a new heart. A few weeks later, maybe a month or so (I do not really recall), he walked in to my office grinning from ear to ear. His eyes were glowing, and he looked up at me and said, "I got a new heart." I remember smiling. I was so happy for him and told him I had heard. I was so happy to see him, and he looked incredible. That is when he looked at me and said, "You didn't listen to what I said. I got a new HEART." As he pounded his fist to his chest, he said, "I got a new heart. God walks with me now." I looked with complete understanding of his new glow. It was not just the transplanted heart. It was God's light that I was witnessing in the new Christian's life.

Another patient slash friend was diagnosed with pancreatic cancer and only had a few months to live. He had been resistant to God's calls in his life. Do not get me wrong, he was a good person, and a few weeks before his death, I got the opportunity to speak to him and asked him if he knew God. He boldly looked at me and said no. I then told him what he already knew, that this cancer is very bad and his days on earth may be numbered, unless God intervenes with some miracle, and he said he did not believe in miracles. I looked at him and said, "You really do not have any other choice!" As our eyes met, I knew God was leading the conversation because this strong man said, "I guess you are right." His son walked up at that moment and said they were ready to go. I learned at his memorial service that was his last time out of his home as from that moment on, he got progressively weaker. I also learned that a very obedient preacher came many times before he died and assured everyone at the service that this man had faith as much as any Christian. His family said that before he died, he had a complete change of heart and accepted God's grace and love. They all noticed a complete change in him as he leaned on God to help him through this horrific disease. The point of this patient's story is to ask every Christian to be bold and let your light shine for God.

While I have been privileged to discuss God with several patients facing life-threatening illnesses, I have also witnessed some individuals whose faith in God never wavered. I was honored to have a nurse named Maria, who I hired because she said she moved from California to our small town because her internet search conveyed that we had the most churches per population. Maria was blessed beyond measure with a voice that rivaled Julie Andrews in the *Sound of Music*. She often would be caught singing "How Do You Solve a Problem like Maria?" She was also an incredible artist. Many of my children and grandchildren have painted portraits by her. All of this talent was bestowed on such a deserving person, but her greatest joy was worshiping God and her beautiful husband, daughter, and son. She was diagnosed with ovarian cancer. What a battle! Through it all, the visits to her always turned out to be a blessing to us, watching her unwavering faith and her love for God and her continued prayers for others. Our local pharmacist said he asked her if there was anything he could do for her, and she said, "Buy the patients in the nursing home a gift for Christmas." Maria got her wish.

Another adorable lady that worked for the clinic for many years was involved in an MVA. My husband and I went to visit her at our adjoining town, and while I never told her this, I did not recognize her. We were both sure that we were in the wrong ICU room until she opened her eyes. Her beautiful eyes were shining through her swollen facial features. She and her husband raised three wonderful children. Her son has served God at home and on foreign soil. God blesses this lady on so many fronts. She has never met a stranger. She could decorate any event, making it more than special, and she smiles with her eyes, knowing that her existence on earth is a blessing from God after allowing her to survive such a horrific accident.

The clinics where we spend the majority of our life has been in existence for over fifty years. My nurse and staff became extended family. It's amazing for me to watch my staff fall in love with our patients. A couple of our nurses have adopted children after caring for them in the clinic. Our family-owned clinic has been a part of many families for generations. As a doctor, I cherish taking caring of the grandchildren of my patients, knowing that at least three generations of this lineage is loyal enough to receive their medical care at our medical establishments.

Recently, while in attendance of a basketball game, my phone rang two different times during this forty-minute game. Looking around, everyone was enjoying the game. While the crowd cheered, I was dealing with medical issues. As my phone rings, one hand covers my ear so I can hear the conversation from the nurse from the hospital and the next phone call from the nursing home. Trying to concentrate as the buzzer is ringing on the game scoreboard is just part of the struggle of being a rural doctor. My husband was rocking a fireplace on one of his days off, and that evening I asked him how his day was, and he responded with "Fine, if I did not have to answer my phone every five minutes." His hands were muddy, making it difficult to get to his phone quick enough. You never want to miss the hospital call because if you do, it is amazing how long it takes to get to the person who was calling upon returning the call. The phone has interrupted countless evening meals with our family, like conversations of the ride home, ball games, homework help, reading bedtime stories, and vacations. Many nights involve at least one phone call. While I am fortunate enough to be able to return to sleep, my husband is not always so fortunate, resulting in many nights with lost sleep. The hours of worrying about patients is countless, yet I cannot imagine doing anything else. Doctors want to please everyone that we can. Maybe we will have to see fifty patients, and everyone goes perfectly, except one. Maybe we just get a very sick patient or a rude, mean patient, and that is all-consuming. Every thought flees to the bad situation. Just when you think you cannot take it another day, a precious patient will bring you homemade cookies, bring you pictures of their daughter's wedding, or share with you the story of how they just had a granddaughter in Minnesota, and she was named after their lovely doctor. The patient had told his daughter that he liked my name, and so her baby carries my name. Wow! How special and sweet. My patients truly become friends. As I record these events, my phone rings with a patient asking a question about her medication. As with almost all conversations, they end the call with "I am sorry to bother you," and I always respond, "No problem. Anytime. Call if you need something."

One of my patients once described my life like a piece of taffy. As she waited and watched patiently on me to enter her room, she said she could not help but notice all the directions that I was stretched that morning. I had her chart in my hand and had tried to enter her room at least half a dozen times, but so many problems had to be answered before I could enter her room. As I reflect on the picture of a stretching piece of taffy, a smile crosses my face in comparing my physician life to a piece of candy. My patients bring joy to me. The richness that each of their shared stories bring to my life is immeasurable. Many share stories of near-death experiences; stories of healing from tobacco abuse, drug addiction, pain, cancer, and depression; the stories of God's presence when they lose a loved one; and the importance of God in times of illness.

The Lord is close to the brokenhearted and saves those who are crushed in spirit. (Psalm 34:18)

He will wipe every tear from their eyes. (Revelation 21:4)

Hearing this, Jesus said to Jairus, "Don't be afraid, just believe, and she will be healed." (Luke 8:50)

Without God's presence, my life as a physician would be grim. Resting on the thought that God is there to help with all illnesses as the great physician helps make the job easier. Bible trivia question: which book of the Bible is written by a physician? Matthew, Mark, Luke, or John? The answer is Luke. To realize that this noble profession has been needed and used by God to help people who are ill since the birth of Jesus is always reassuring when I reflect on my career path. I often wonder what I will do in heaven since there will be no more pain or sickness. What an awesome thought. I have seen enough suffering on earth.

While life as a rural doctor is rewarding, the biggest rewards still lie with my personal life, and that includes my family. My parents, husband, children, grandchildren, and extended family circle is where my life's true joy occurs. Our private holiday gatherings hold such special memories for all of us. While many may consider this rural life boring, we love our cabin life. A sweet girl who shares my birthday wrote a perfect description of our time around a campfire laughing and talking. She described the times as memories that remind us of just how blessed we are to have lifelong friends to share experiences of life.

CHAPTER 6

Lilliona Grace

"Lily of the Valley"

"He is the lily of the valley, the bright and morning star,
he is the fairest of ten thousand to my soul."

Like a lily among the thorns, so is my darling
among the maidens. (Song of Songs 2:2)

"Amazing Grace"

"Amazing grace, how sweet the sound that saved a wretch like me."

For by grace you have been saved through faith. And this is
not your own doing; it is the gift of God. (Ephesians 2:8)

God created Lilliona Grace for us to cherish. Her radiant smile and beautiful blue eyes sparkle with kindness. She loves life. As we watch her bloom, we are reminded of how lucky we are to be chosen to be on this journey with this unique, unpredictable, innocent, incredible child. She can be hardheaded and trying as any child ever created, but what joy she brings to my heart at the thought of her precious life.

When Lilly was around two or three years old, we had an upcoming court date to decide guardianship. The court was going to decide her fate on a Monday morning. The Sunday before this frightful day, I sat in church streaming tears, and the music leader had picked two songs for this morning's service. They were "Lily of the Valley" and "Amazing Grace." What peace I felt listening to those songs written so many years ago. To think that the authors of the songs were obedient to God's nudging and really had no idea that years later God would use them to give me peace in rural Oklahoma. The music director obviously followed God's lead as well. I am sure she thought that she picked these songs, but she did not. God did, and she was obedient to His urging. While "Amazing Grace" is sung often in our church, to my knowledge, "Lily of the Valley" has not been sung since that day. To all the music leaders, your job is so important, and God uses you for someone in every service that you serve.

Lilly has been such a giving child. I hope this continues throughout her life. On her first year of school, I took her Christmas shopping for her teacher. She wanted to bring all her classmates something, and she did not stop there. She wanted to get all the cooks and the cafeteria workers something because she loved the food they made for her every day. Therefore, we got them all a box of chocolates and have since then made it a tradition to remember them at Christmas. They smile and seem generally happy when they get this small gesture of gratitude. Having a grandchild is one of the most incredible blessings ever to be bestowed on someone, and I am lucky enough to have eleven so far. Just when I thought my kids were grown and I was going to be bored, Lilliona's arrival changed that thought. Lilly's parents were very young teenagers when she was born. Lilly's mom and I talk often and have become friends. My prayer life includes prayers for her and her daughter, Jimma, who is Lilly's half-sister. God places people in your life for a reason. Sometimes we wonder why. I remember being so distraught when I learned my young son was having a child. One of my dear employees, Debbie, noticed how upset I was over the situation and said crazy things like "This is going to be okay" and "This baby is going to be your biggest blessing." I was half-laughing, thinking to myself that there is no way this is going to be okay, but again I was so wrong. I had no idea that I would be raising this beautiful child. My husband and I became legal guardians when she was about six months old, and our sleeping through the night was over for a couple of years. Good thing we had so much practice with our usual nightly hospital calls. When Lilly was only five years old, I started teaching her Bible verses. She learned verses like John 3:16 ("For God so loved the world that he gave his only begotten son so whoever believed in Him shall not perish, but have everlasting life") and Psalm 23:1 ("The Lord is my shepherd, I lack nothing") and Philippians 4:13 ("I can do all things through Christ who strengthens me"). As I remember these verses, I wonder which one God will use in her life as her comfort verse!

Shortly after Lilly came into our life, my husband's father passed away, and he often said that the only way he survived this painful moment was knowing he had to help Lilly. Lilliona was just a baby, and yet her presence helped fill an emptiness in our hearts. It was God's perfect timing. He knows what we need even before we have any idea we will be needing something. My father-in-law was also a doctor, and he was one of the best. He practiced medicine when doctors were heroes. He worked day and night at the sacrifice of his own life. His four boys loved him unconditionally. He had a way of making you feel like the most special person in the world. His loss was not only as that of a father but also a medical partner. This family medical business was dependent on his wisdom, and without his advice and experience, it was hard to continue. My husband stepped up to the plate and filled those large shoes to keep the business running even today. Lilly was instrumental in keeping my husband focused when he really wanted to give up. She would say some of the cutest comments, keeping us laughing and smiling at the same time. It is truly amazing to watch all my grandchildren blossom with their own unique personalities. How can God create each and every one as a one of a kind creation? Anyone that is an artist or an author knows how difficult it is to write a new story or create a new painting, but just imagine creating new life since time began, and everyone is exactly how He intended us to be. Each one is a perfect masterpiece, and each with their very own genetics. Time flies so quickly with children and grandchildren. It has already been a decade since Lilly's birth, and I can remember it like it was yesterday. Since this our second time around the block, we have a real perception of just how fast time marches in a child's life. We stay busy with piano lessons, dance practice, basketball, softball, soccer, and 4-H. Lilly was not blessed with the greatest athletic abilities, but she has always wanted to try. She loves all water sports like swimming, water skiing, inner tubing, and knee boarding. She is also a good downhill snow skier (the faster the better) and is already driving a four-wheeler up our mountain cliff road. We sandwich her between the lead four-wheeler, and someone takes up the rear on another four-wheeler. She does have a gift of public speaking because she can memorize and she is not afraid to get up in front of a crowd. Some children are blessed with talents for everything; others have to have help in finding the talent they possess. The grade school principal came up to me after a gifted and talented program and stated that Lilly should join 4-H to compete in public speaking. If she had not made the effort to talk to me about Lilly's talent, I might never have noticed. She competed in 4-H and placed at the state contest on her first year in 4-H. Our children get so many negative comments, so I encourage every parent, teacher, and friend to compliment a child whenever you can. An advice I would pass on to all parents is to cherish every moment with your children. I was so busy with work that I feel like I missed so many little events. My children loved Friday because that was the day I would try to get off work early enough to pick them up from school. What a joy to see their smiling faces walking to the car and so excited to go to the Sonic to get a drink or ice cream after school snack. For them, the small things were as important as the big moments. Lilly and the rest of the grandchildren seem to be the same way. Riding bikes at the lake, camping on the cliff, or playing Sorry! board games brought us together for great memories. My prayer for Lilliona continues to include peace in her life, perfect mate picked by God himself, and lots of smiles and laughter along the way. God's gift of a child is a blessing from heaven. Pray for your children's protection, future, friends, and salvation. Nothing is more important than your children's personal relationship with God.

CHAPTER 7

Gift of Children

"As for me, this is my covenant with them," says the Lord. "My spirit, who is in you, will not depart from you and my words that I have put in your mouth will always be on the lips of your children, and the lips of their descendants—from this time and forever," says the Lord. "Arise, shine, for your light has come, and the glory of the Lord rises upon you." (Isaiah 59:21–22)

Every good gift and every perfect gift is from above, coming down from the father. (James 1:17)

My sons Lance, Jeff, and Danny have brought untold joy to my life. Lance was my firstborn, and the gift of this baby was phenomenal. He's been used by God and loves riding motorcycles. He even got his motorcycle license before he was old enough to get a driver's license. He had a dog named Bear that followed his every move. Obviously, none of my children are perfect and struggle with making good life choices, Lance may have been my most caring child. He actually worked as an undertaker for a while, and when I hear stories of him actually carrying a lifeless baby in the morgue instead of rolling her in on the cold steel bed, a small tear falls from my eye knowing he has a heart that can be tapped by God. As a mother, I say endless prayers for his life.

My sons Jeff and Dan complete our family's boys. They all love guns and motorcycles. We took a couple of family vacations on the back of a motorcycle. Yellowstone is an amazing vacation spot, especially when riding on a motorcycle. The smells, the weather (from hot to sleet in less than a few hours), and the fear of the buffalo within arm's length away as they cross the road in front of you all make the experience unforgettable. While our family are not avid hunters, the boys all love guns. If fact, Dan was an incredible skeet shooter in high school. They all played football, so we spent many Friday nights attending football games and watching one of the boys. Jeff learned to fly before he graduated from high school. His high school graduation present was his very own airplane. He is a professional pilot to this day. The other two boys went into the medical business. One takes X-rays, and one is an ultrasound technician. Jeff, along with his precious wife who is a nurse practitioner, are blessed with two wonderful boys. They love their adventures in rural Oklahoma mountains, chasing Bigfoot, riding four-wheelers, shooting BB guns, and spending special time with Bus Grandpa. My husband got the name because our visits to their home are usually done in our motor home, hence the driver of a bus.

Dan has blessed us with our youngest granddaughter and with our oldest. When he visits, the girls are definitely the majority. All three girls are beautiful and uniquely different. Another blessing that God has bestowed on our family was when little Vivian was found at the bottom of a backyard swimming pool, blue and lifeless. Her mom and dad had perfect timing to get her rescued and start CPR before the EMS arrived to continue this heroic effort. She is perfect, and we give God all the glory for what could have been our family's worse disaster ever.

The blessing of my daughter is more than can be recorded. She was born at the end of July in the extreme heat of an Oklahoma summer. My extra fifty pounds made me extremely happy when she finally decided to arrive. She was my second birth, and I was a doctor, so I knew what to expect in this delivery process. Understand that this was several decades ago, and I wanted to have a natural childbirth. I did not even know the sex of the baby, but I knew in my heart that I was having a girl. Several hours into labor, fear struck as I realized that things were not going exactly smoothly. I had been pushing for quite some time, and nothing was happening. I even remember saying to my husband that I wanted to talk to my mom because I thought I might be dying. Obviously, I was not, but it felt strange, and finally I delivered a ten-pound, fifteen-ounce baby girl. This girl was nicknamed Lastly by her brothers and brought so much joy to our family. She, to this day, lights up a room when she enters. As with all children, we went through ups and downs through the years. One year, she was pitcher of the softball team, and the next year she did not even play. One year, she made cheerleading squad, and the next year she did not.

As I watched my middle school beautiful, talented daughter be defeated when she did not make the cheer team, I knew we had to do something to show her just how beautiful she really was both inside and out. Therefore, we discussed options, and she said she would like to join a pageant. Are you kidding? Instead of saying what I thought, I said okay. Believe me, I knew nothing about pageants, and she entered her first pageant in the Oklahoma National American Miss pageant system. This pageant has some things that you can do, like selling ads in the program to ensure your child gets a crown. We were certainly not rich, but I made sure that enough ads were sold so that she would not come home empty-handed. The process of pageantry was perfect for us. We went shopping to look for the perfect outfits.

We practiced speeches and introductions. We learned current events for the interview portion of the pageant. Obviously, we loved the photo sessions, hair and makeup, and modeling practices. At every pageant, we had our dear friend Misty by our side to help keep us organized and Leslie totally polished when she entered the stage.

The first pageant was a success. She placed in the top five out of eighty-ish girls. The bug had hit her. She won many awards, but most importantly, she got her confidence back. The following year, there were one hundred seventy six girls in her age division. My daughter won many awards at this event. She won speech, acting, best photo, and first runner-up overall. But what I remember most as I walked onstage to greet my daughter was a grandmother hugging her granddaughter who had made it to the top five, saying "God has great things in store for you." I walked over to my daughter thinking the same thing. God has great things planned for your life. I remember one pageant in particular in Los Angles, California, where the contestants were required to introduce their mom. The crowd was very large, and as we stood at the podium, my daughter spoke with such grace and authority as my legs were trembling just standing there with her.

At her high school graduation, she turned to me and smiled so beautifully and just gave me a little wave. Tears poured! Decades later, as I reflect on this moment, tears still will flow down my face. My best friend leaving home was almost more than I could bare, but with God and my husband being supportive through all the tears, I survived this empty nest time. Little did I know God had one of my biggest blessings arriving soon, another daughter/granddaughter. Lilly was on the way to help fill my nest. She is really my granddaughter but calls me Mom half the time.

My daughter and her husband have two perfect blessings. Their children glow with God's love. Little Blakelee's nightly prayers always include my knee by saying "Don't forget Nannie's knee!" That simple prayer keeps me smiling. She loves to try on my high heels and is like all little princesses when it comes to makeup and nail polish. Little Landry, all boy, loves to scare me by jumping out from behind the door, and his infectious laugh keeps me grinning from ear to ear.

The Bible refers to our grandchildren as the crown of the elderly. My grandsons Aidan, Landry, Grant, and Kasey and my granddaughters Payton, Lilliona, Kyleigh, Blakelee, Vivian, Dovie, and Jimma bring joy to our blended family beyond words could describe. If you are seasoned enough to be blessed with grandchildren, many will agree with the old cliché that you love your grandchildren as much as your own children. It is true.

Being raised as a doctor's child in a small town has both advantages and disadvantages. As mentioned earlier, they had to share their time with countless patients. When the phone rang, they immediately knew to be quiet, and whatever we were doing would have to wait until the phone call was finished. My father-in-law started our family medical business half a century ago. This practice now employs our two sons who are taking X-rays and doing ultrasounds. My daughter and her husband help by managing our chronic care patients. My father-in-law had four boys, and three of them are directly involved in patient care. My husband is a family practice doctor. His brother is a dentist in our shared office space, and his wife is an excellent teacher at our local school. Their daughter, my lovely niece has dedicated her life to children's ministry. His other brother is a world champion rodeo heeler and works as the hospital administrator. He is married to our town's physical therapist. My brother's beautiful family including my sister-in law who is an LPN at the clinic, and my beautiful nieces, my children's cousin, and my nieces' friends from college work every summer and break from school to help with whatever needs to be caught up at the time from billing to the front desk. My other brother-in-law is a preacher and his wife is a teacher. They stay busy chasing after five wonderful children. From my grandparents to first cousins, we come from almost all walks of life—welders, nurses, teachers, preachers, rodeo stars, PTs (physical therapists), NP, X-ray technicians, pilots, bankers, lawyers, janitors, diner waitresses, hospital administrators, doctors, dentists, cross fit coaches, business managers, super secretaries, tax assessor, counselors, ranchers, veterinarians, TV anchors, sports broadcasters, and college students. My family, while centrally located in Oklahoma, extends also to Colorado, New Mexico, Texas, Illinois, Iowa, Nebraska, New

Jersey, Connecticut, Florida, South Dakota, and Kansas. We are scattered all throughout the United States. Many have followed the lead of God and work in the ministry field. Some work as priests, nuns, music directors, associate pastors, youth directors, and Sunday school teachers, and some have gone on mission trips to Africa and on world tours to help spread the gospel. Our family has also had many prayer chains whenever someone in the family is facing any trial. Without this support system, I cannot imagine facing all of life's difficulties. God is there for you whether you ask for yourself or call on the whole crew and involve everyone to pray. The Bible states that we should not lay up treasures on earth, where moth and rust doth corrupt and where thieves break and steal, but instead lay up treasures in heaven.

Children are a blessing from God. Whether you deliver, inherit, or adopt, God wants and expects us to protect and nurture all the children. I certainly have failed my children on many fronts, but one thing is very consistent, I pray for them all. I believe and have said this to many parents that are heartbroken with children who make bad choices: God absolutely answers the prayer of parents or grandparents praying for their child's salvation. I ask God to never stop knocking on my children's hearts until they are saved and come to heaven with me. Every single one of my children, myself included, has made bad choices. Some have broken my heart. God alone can bring salvation to your child, but we as parents have an obligation to pray for our children. Having a large family makes you realize everyone is unique. Everyone is different. Some are so easy, others are normal by the world's standards, and others are so hard. I have children of all types, but from the hardest to the easiest, all make our family complete, and I want all to be with me in eternity.

CHAPTER 8

Seasons of Time

There is a time for everything and a season for every
activity under the heavens. (Ecclesiastes 3:1)

Wait for the LORD; be strong and take heart
and wait for the LORD. (Psalm 27:14)

How many have complained about God's timing? He takes too long to answer our prayers, so we try to handle the situation ourselves. In Proverbs 16:9, it says, "In their hearts humans plan their course, but the Lord establishes their steps." God has a purpose for everything in our life. As I look around this beautiful October morning, with the hardwood leaves turning the most incredible colors, I reflect on the fact that the leaves are dying, yet it is their most beautiful time. Obviously, spring is a great season as well. When the leaves sprout a new youthful green and young flowers bloom, renewed energy is ever so present. Young children, blooming and energetic, are the spring of life. The summer comes as midlife. Nice times, but you have a job to do. It reminds me of the season of worker bees. So many times during this time, we do not ever look up. We just work and take care of the children, house, and bills, and then it is fall. The aches and pains start, but it is in this season that you are the most beautiful. Just like the red leaves of the maple trees, your knowledge is vast, and you have seen the spring and survived the summer.

My childhood was fun. I had special times playing outside with my brother and cousins. We rode horses, bikes, and motorcycles. We made mud pies, jumped rope, picked wild blackberries on the side of our dirt road, gathered lots of eggs, and laughed a lot. I loved school. Both of my parents were teachers and always stressed the importance of doing your best. I thought I could go to school forever, but by the time I finished medical school, I was ready to start a new phase of my life—work!

Thirty years on a job that is essentially twenty-four seven dominates my life (my summer season). During this entire thirty-year-span, the longest vacation taken at one time was one and three-fourths weeks at one time! A few times, we have taken ten days (one week and both weekends around the week). Almost all vacations have included calls to discuss a patient, a hospital concern, or a staff issue. Peppered with the stressful job is some of my most cherished memories of family gatherings, vacations, and frequent camping trips. Most of our vacations were road trips to national parks. America is beautiful! Each national park is uniquely spectacular.

As I enter the golden years, life feels like it is flying. Time is a priceless gift! During my busy career, I often wondered what people who are retired did all day. As you age, your mind has plans of everything that you will accomplish for the day, but somehow your body does not work as fast, and so you have to learn to pace yourself.

Recently my son called me at 2:30 a.m. and asked for help. He had been drinking and needed me to come pick him up. When I arrived, he had several friends with him who also needed to be brought home. Therefore, I brought them to my house and told them all to be ready at 7:30 a.m. since that is when I would be leaving to go to work. At 7:28 a.m., when I looked out the window, I saw that one of our vehicles was missing. An employee of mine arrived at the house at 7:30 a.m. and said he had just met the truck in the driveway. In no way am I comparing myself to God's grace and goodness, but the parent in me was thinking about my son and his friends. I was wondering what to get them for breakfast.

My son was running because he did not want to face me. What a mistake! Yes, he would receive a harsh lecture of how it is not okay to be drinking in public and how wrong it is to risk people's lives. By running, he was driving in a stolen vehicle, making another bad choice. How different his day would have been if he had stayed put instead of running. God laid on my heart that we should turn all problems to prayer. Wait on Him; do not try to handle it yourself. He has grace, forgiveness, love, and a solution to your problem. His answers and solutions are much better than you can even imagine.

Wait on the Lord! Trust with every fiber of your soul. God will bless you for obeying this command. My life has been a series of trials, and just when I was at the top of my game, my career was struck as well.

CHAPTER 9

Destruction at Work

The thief comes only to steal and kill and destroy; I came that they may have life, and have it abundantly. (John 10:10)

I have been blessed with more than can be recorded on the pages of any book. I have had my share of tests with divorce, tornadoes, floods, MVA, miscarriage, robbery, health issues, nearly drowning, and loss of loved ones, but when tragedy struck my job, I was devastated. With all these events, I really believe God was with me and giving me the assurance to muddle through these life crisis situations. It is so hard to stay worry-free when some tragedies strikes your family or career. I was working very hard every day and was at the top of my career when some auditing firm decided that I was not worthy of seeing patients for Medicaid anymore. I was more than devastated. As I am traumatized by a medical legal action taken against me, God is prompting me to go outside to read my Bible. A few months earlier, God laid on my heart to read the Bible from cover to cover. He did this by sending patients to me (again those obedient children of God) one after another. Each patient had his or her own story of how important it is to read the Bible from the beginning to the end. Amazingly enough, after I started this process, not another patient mentioned reading the Bible in this way. I assume God had other things to focus on after I became obedient and opened the Bible on page one. While I had read many passages in the Bible, I had never started like this and immediately started getting bogged down with the names in Genesis. When I would feel like giving up, I would remember that I had a chemistry degree. Strange words can be conquered. I wrote out a family tree and studied as I was going be quizzed by my high school or college chemistry teachers. I tried to read some every day, and as with all things at first, I was very diligent, but then life would get busy, and I could only read every couple of days. I say this because I believe God's timing is perfect. He needed me to be on the exact page that I was reading when tragedy struck my thirty-year career. With complete devastation, I can barely concentrate as I open my Bible to read. My eyes filled with tears, and I cannot even see the words clearly. "Go outside to read." How silly! It is the end of June, and it is hot in Oklahoma. "Go outside to read." Therefore, for some reason, I put my shoes on and went outside. It was hot, and there was no wind. I open my Bible to the book of Jeremiah, right where I had left off, but the wind lifted up a single page and turned it. I would gently put it back down, and then the single page lifted repeatedly, and on the fourth time, I actually turned the page to read what was on that page. Now remember, I had read this page a few days before, but as I read it this day, it became alive for me. Such comforting words spoken just for me. That day, the words were super powerful for me. After I read chapter fifteen, I turned back where I had left off and resumed my daily reading. There was no wind, and my page did not turn again. I even tested the situation and took both hands off the Bible and waited. No turning page.

God is the one with perfect timing, and as I wait for His answer, I go forward waiting anxiously for what He has in store for me. As we go through trials and suffering, I often ask and wonder why. God is present and has prepared you to deal with every crossroad in life. I suppose if everything was perfect on earth, we might not turn to God and might forget to rely on our sovereign God. As I pray daily for God's answer to this situation, I asked God to let me receive a call to end this Medicaid ordeal. While with my eighty-year-old dad was recovering from cardiac bypass surgery, I received a call from the governor's office asking me to be on a physician manpower board that had to have senate confirmation. I was excited and, of course, said I would love to be placed on the board. Understand that I did not apply for this position. I filled the application and had my interview, and everything was perfect until I told them about the Medicaid review. A few minutes after, I get a call that the governor might be embarrassed if the news made it to the senate floor. I said that I understood and, of course, was crushed. I did not ask for the appointment. I did not know the governor, and so I wish I would have said the response my husband gave when he said, "Well, he is making a big mistake because you would have been perfect for the position."

> Rejoice in this, though now for a short time
> you have had to struggle in various trials. (1 Peter
> 1:6)

God allows trials to refine the Christian so that when tragedy strikes, our faith is tested and made strong. Throughout my life, God has given me strong signs to reassure me. Obviously, a very strong, faithful Christian that does not require so much coddling is blessed as the Bible eludes that those who believe even though they do not see him (blind faith) are more blessed.

> You love him, though you have not seen him. Though not seeing him now, you believe in him and rejoice with inexpressible and glorious joy. (1 Peter 1:8)

For the duration of the trial, I have cried and felt so alone and generally sad. God sends daily scripture through my family, friends and coworkers who are God's obedient Christians. These up lifting prayers have truly helped my survival of the event. However, God says that I should one day be filled with joy. How? The only way is standing on the certainty that God is here holding my hand. I will grow and be refined with this trial. Therefore, to walk closer with God, I endure the burden of the trial. God will win all battles, and He stands beside me through the storm. As if this is not enough, my dad develops chest pain, and the fight for his life begins.

CHAPTER 10

Prayer

I call on you, my God, for you will answer me; turn
your ear to me and hear my prayer. (Psalm 17:6)

As my father lay in the ICU bed after his perfectly performed surgery, while receiving incredible care, I called on many prayer warriors. I contacted my preacher patients, my church, and my family and friends. People from several states and almost every religion lifted a prayer to heaven for my dad. I had my dear friend call an active eighty-six-year-old preacher patient of mine to pray, and he did. When I thanked him later for his prayers, he was very quick to take no credit and said, "Don't thank me. Thank God." He has been a preacher for forty-six years and has seen many things in his life as a pastor. He even thought about writing a book. He even bought a typewriter but thought no one would want to read anything he wrote. I sat there smiling, thinking the same thing about me writing a book. Tell me to take a chemistry course or learn to teach a science class, but use my English skills to write a book? You are kidding, right? Yet I am prompted almost daily to write this conglomerate of memories and hope that someone will see God's light in their lives and hearts as they toil through life. My preacher friend does not realize how rich his testimony is to me. He told me about his son, who was born in just fifteen minutes at the local hospital. His church was having a revival. After his son was born, he attended the revival, and two days later, his son attended his first church service. Needless to say, his son has grown up with a praying father and mother. What a blessing to any child! Yet another of my preacher patients did not start out so lucky in life. She describes her childhood with quite a bit different beginning. She said that they were poor and lived in a house with dirt floors. She was a product of incest of her teenage mother. Her mother left home when she was thirteen or fourteen, leaving this future preacher with her grandmother and grandfather, who was actually her father. She is on fire for God and often starts our medical visit with a prayer. I have had many other preachers through my practice, all with a special place in my heart. I have so many praying patients that I cannot even begin to write about each one of them. One patient was recently diagnosed with stage four cancer, and as I look at him, lost for words, he said that he had never walked closer with God, and when he cannot walk anymore, God will carry him. I shared this with another family member facing the fear of aggressive cancer, and he assured me that he knew Jesus and was leaning on Him. One of my patients told me that she never forgets to talk to God by setting a timer on her phone, which reminds her if she had not prayed in a few hours. Another patient boldly confessed that he is ready to be used by God to give a testimony of salvation. I asked him if he was a preacher, and he said that he could not be a pastor because he had been divorced a couple of times. He was always willing to preach anytime someone needed a service or two.

God uses the perfect and the imperfect. Do not let your mistakes keep you away from God as I did for so many years. Prayer is a powerful tool. God loves us and wants us to walk around with a grateful, thankful heart. The Bible holds the answers for your life.

> Now may the Lord of peace Himself give
> you peace always in every way. The Lord be with
> you all. (2 Thessalonians 3:16, NKJV)

The tornado, the flood, the MVA, the illness, the pain and suffering, the loss, the fear of thieves, the divorce, the fight of obesity, the miscarriages, the failures at work, the disappointments, and anything else that is thrown at you by the destroying angel (a.k.a. Satan) can be overcome by the one true God. Jesus gave the ultimate sacrifice so we will be victorious. Peace to all from our Lord and Savior, Jesus Christ.

Every trial that comes your way is used by God to refine you, to make you more readily available to be used by God. When we are born, God has a purpose for our life. He gives you free will but will nudge you where He wants your life to lead. Follow the nudging. Listen to the sweet, still voice in your soul. It is my wish that you read these words realizing your life is not so different from mine. Your trials might be different, but look for God's presence through them all. Turn to Him to fix your problems as He gives you the desires of your heart. As I am approaching the fall of my life (the most beautiful time), I encourage you to include God early in your life. The reward is endless—eternity in heaven.

As I am preparing to attend Blakelee's fifth birthday, I realize I have been writing this book for five years, recording events and God's presence. One last thought in Ezekiel 33:16, it says, "None of the sins that a person committed will be remembered against them. Do what is just and right and you will surely live." Every saved Christian's sins are forgiven, but even more, they are forgotten. They are completely erased by the blood of Jesus Christ.

The world is full of trials, but the gift of life—well, so worth the trip or the journey. Every single day, God provides something for you to be thankful. You are blessed because you are a child of God.

About the Author

My name is Dr. Victoria Rowland, and I am a rural Oklahoma family physician practicing in one of the poorest towns in America. My career of thirty years has all been served in our little corner of the world. Married with a blended family of five children and ten grandchildren, love for family and work are what keep me smiling. "Lord, let me help at least one person today" is my motto and daily prayer while traveling to work. My hobbies include photo memory books, traveling, and going on camping vacations where everyone in the family is present. I pray for God's blessings to pour out abundantly on you.

CPSIA information can be obtained
at www.ICGtesting.com
Printed in the USA
LVHW091200311220
675393LV00007B/1160